At the Top of Their Game

Richard Sherman

Shutting Down and Speaking Up

Ruth Bjorklund

Cavendish Square

New York

Published in 2018 by Cavendish Square Publishing, LLC
243 5th Avenue, Suite 136, New York, NY 10016

Library of Congress Cataloging-in-Publication Data

Names: Bjorklund, Ruth.
Title: Richard Sherman : shutting down and speaking up / Ruth Bjorklund.
Description: New York : Cavendish Square, 2018. | Series: At the top of their game | Includes index.
Identifiers: ISBN 9781502628312 (library bound) | ISBN 9781502628428 (ebook)
Subjects: LCSH: Sherman, Richard, 1988-. | Football players--United States--Biography.
Classification: LCC GV939.S44 B56 2018 | DDC 796.332092--dc23

Editorial Director: David McNamara
Editor: Fletcher Doyle
Copy Editor: Rebecca Rohan
Associate Art Director: Amy Greenan
Designer: Jessica Nevins
Production Coordinator: Karol Szymczuk
Photo Research: J8 Media

Printed in the United States of America

At the Top of Their Game

Contents

Who Is Richard Sherman?

From a neighborhood where people are wary to walk alone, even during the day, and avoid it at all costs at night, came a young man who made plans to leave town, and to leave it in style. His style, Richard Sherman's style, is bold, brash, and brilliant. But for all his success, he never forgot where he came from.

Richard Sherman is a famous (or infamous, depending on who is talking) National Football League (NFL) **cornerback** for the Seattle Seahawks. Rarely is an NFL defensive player a household name, but Richard Sherman has made his mark, loud and clear. He plays with speed and athleticism and is an avid student of the game. He is dogged, and vocal, in his pursuit of excellence.

As a youth, Richard Sherman was a go-getter. His plans for a future in professional football not only included developing his exceptional athletic skills, but getting the best education possible. In his community, where gangs were in control, brute force over brains was the rule of law. Ignoring any lure of the streets, Richard Sherman set his goals and aimed high. He worked hard, attending inner-city

Opposite: Richard Sherman has become the face of the Seattle Seahawks' secondary from his cornerback position.

public schools and studying from textbooks nearly a decade old. His diligence and intellect earned him a scholarship to one of the top universities in the country.

Football was the plan, but Richard also played basketball and baseball, and ran track and field. He set school records and won state titles in track and field. As a versatile football player who inspired others with his energy, he propelled his high school football team into the upper ranks of its division. In college, he continued

Sherman is popular with sportswriters and other media reporters who appreciate his humorous and insightful interviews.

his success, being instrumental in turning a losing team into a national champion.

Richard was drafted as a professional player after college. He did not come into the game quietly. Working his way up as a rookie from reserve to starter, he talked the whole way. Richard was, and is, a big talker. He is known for nonstop trash-talking on the field but encouraging chatter with teammates, and funny, intelligent, and sometimes very intense interviews with the media.

Richard Sherman is part of a fierce and dominating defensive team. As a vital member of the Seahawks' **secondary**, he is known, and counted on, for the big plays. He is passionate on the field, on the sidelines, on the practice field, and in his personal life.

A game-winner in more ways than one, Richard Sherman, young as he is, has left a legacy for many to learn from and to follow. He is generous with his time and his money, and he spreads his good fortune onto others. He visits schools to deliver inspiring and encouraging speeches, he provides for the needy in his community and in his troubled hometown, and he seeks out young people who want to achieve but are challenged because of the lack of basic necessities. He ardently supports his teammates, his family, and those less advantaged than he is. On the field and off, Richard Sherman is a man to admire.

The Early Years

Chapter 1

If you ask people, especially Seattle Seahawks fans, about Richard Sherman's childhood, they immediately respond, "He grew up in Compton." True, Sherman did grow up in the Los Angeles suburb of Compton and as many know, Compton, California can be a tough place to live. But Richard Sherman's childhood was influenced by more than geography; he grew up with a family, a strong, hardworking family.

Richard Sherman was born on March 30, 1988. He was a happy addition to the family as he joined his parents, Beverly and Kevin, and three-year-old brother Branton. Especially in those early years, their neighborhood was a dangerous place. There were drugs and gangs and turf wars and poverty, but Sherman's parents were determined to protect their sons and send them into the world, each ready to be his own man.

Sherman insists he was only seven years old when he decided he was going to play football in the NFL. "I kind of locked it in," he said. "That was it when they told me, 'Man, they *pay* football players to

Opposite: This abandoned and graffiti-covered house is one of many such houses in the neighborhood where Sherman grew up.

play the game!'" When Sherman learned that Deion Sanders, a star cornerback and first-round draft pick, was signed to a multimillion-dollar contract, he decided football was the life for him. He may have set himself up with a mission in life, but he got his chance to live that dream because of his parents. Sherman gives his parents full credit for their devoted perseverance and his success.

Sherman's obstacles, caused by living in a troubled city, were very real and very present. His first years were spent in Watts, a city ravaged by poverty, crime, and attention-grabbing riots. When the Sherman family moved to nearby Compton, it was considered a hotbed of American inner-city violence and despair. In 1988, the

During Sherman's childhood years, Compton was a city faced with many challenges, including poverty, gangs, and crime.

rap group NWA (Dr. Dre, Ice-T, and Easy-E) released an album that took the music industry and the country by storm. It was titled *Straight Outta Compton*. The songs reflected the rage and rebellion of young black men with few opportunities to escape the cycle of poverty. Their music described the culture of Compton as especially drug-infested, desperate, and violent. The group's message to the outside world was that anybody who could live and survive in Compton was someone to be respected and feared. Compton was by no means the only city in America with such problems, but it was the city with the worst reputation. It was in that context that Beverly and Kevin Sherman were faced with the challenge of making a good life for themselves and their children.

Wake-Up Call

Kevin Sherman was an athlete in high school with high hopes of seeing where in the world his athleticism could take him. But in a stroke of bad luck, he was involved in a go-kart accident and lost an eye. Losing an eye gave him the sense that he was not going anywhere in life. He lost his drive and his self-confidence. He was arrested for truancy and started hanging around with gang members. He was not an official member, but he was no stranger to the gang's illegal activities and violence. When he was eighteen, he was hanging around with some gang members when a car pulled up full of rival gang members who were armed with guns. Kevin was caught in the crossfire of bullets and was shot twice in the chest. It was a turning point for him. As the saying goes, he was scared straight. "After that," he said, "I needed to get my act together … I went out and got a job and I've worked ever since." He worked in a number of low-paying jobs until he was hired by the Los Angeles Public Works

Department as a sanitation worker. In the early days, he said it was "gross and horrendous, and very humbling," but, he continued, "To me, it didn't matter. It was the price I had to pay to feed my family." Each day, Kevin Sherman woke up at 3:45 a.m. to go and collect garbage. He has done so now for more than thirty years.

Kevin Sherman's work ethic made a huge impression on Richard and Branton. It would have been easy enough for the boys to fall in with the neighborhood troublemakers. And for a time, Branton did. But whenever Kevin Sherman saw his sons heading in the wrong direction, he pulled them back. "I couldn't let the same thing happen to them," he said. So, he would call them over, take off his shirt, and show them the scars from his bullet wounds. As Richard Sherman said recently, "I think it was incredibly significant. It forced my brother and me to understand priorities and family. You've got to do everything in your power to make sure your family is taken care of."

Beverly Sherman, whom Kevin credits with turning his life around, had an enormous and positive influence on her children. She was a loving and energetic mother who did not stand for nonsense from her children. She was clear about her expectations. She encouraged both of her sons to stay involved with sports, believing if they were successful at sports it would detract from the allure of gangs and keep them away from youngsters in the thrall of gangs. She refused to allow them to wear gang colors—red for Bloods, blue for Crips. She impressed upon them the importance of schoolwork. She began paying her children five dollars for every A on their report cards, and three dollars for every B. Richard liked the pocket money, but eventually he caught on to his mother's real motivation.

Beverly Sherman worked with intellectually and physically disabled children for California Children's Services. When Richard was seven, she took him to work on Take Your Child to Work Day. Richard was unprepared. He recalled later that the experience was "surreal, a whole different world." What he soon saw was how much hope and energy her young students displayed while learning to do tasks that Richard took for granted. He admired their patience and the patience of their therapists, parents, and caregivers as they achieved each milestone, each personal victory. He was also impressed with children facing life-threatening diseases who lived their lives with bravery and a positive attitude. Richard befriended many of the children and frequently returned on his own to play games, chat, read stories out loud, and be a friend. He learned from them the philosophy that every day is a gift, and there are no guarantees. Richard saw in real time what his mother had always taught him about respecting others and not judging them for what they cannot control—such as a disability or the color of their skin. Again, like her husband, Beverly Sherman taught her children by example. Their lessons were not wasted on their children. As Richard said later, "Growing up in Compton, I needed parents like mine."

Richard and Branton were fun-loving boys. It was not unusual for their mother to come home and find them "whooping it up" around the living room. Of course, sometimes there might be a tipped-over table, a broken lamp, maybe a small hole punched in the wall. What would follow would be the expectation that they would repair the damage and replace the loss. More than anything there would be forgiveness and a clean slate. Both parents knew that they had passionate and energetic children, and they knew that their energy would come to be one of their greatest assets.

Making It

The Sherman brothers both had faith they would make it big. They looked forward to a bright future with confidence, despite their surroundings. They often marched around the house pretending to be in victory parades. Branton recalls trooping around their bedrooms carrying imaginary Super Bowl and NBA (National Basketball Association) championship trophies on their heads. Branton said he always got the MVP (Most Valuable Player) trophy because he was the oldest. The boys spent a lot of time together. They cracked jokes and horsed around a lot. "You had to get on them to tone it down," said their mother. Both Richard and Branton wished that they had fewer household rules and more freedom. Most of the kids in their neighborhood did. But Kevin and Beverly felt that it was their duty to watch out for their sons closely. They believed in discipline. The children—the boys now had a younger sister named Krystina—were not allowed to take the bus or walk too far from home. If any of the children were caught hanging around someone questionable, they were told to go home and read a book or practice throwing a ball.

The Shermans would chauffeur the children to parties and then sit in the car and wait outside. Richard recalls that it was embarrassing. Beverly was so passionate about protecting her children that the local gang members could do little else but respect her. In fact, many of them took to keeping a watchful eye on Richard and his siblings. Kevin was equally committed to being a good parent. Richard was often at his side at home problem-solving and learning skills from his father, such as repairing broken plumbing, building a fence, or fixing a car. Kevin recalls that Richard was an extremely curious child.

Proud parents Beverly and Kevin Sherman have decorated their home with photos and memorabilia from Richard's football career.

Richard, known today for being a big talker, started young. Said Branton, "This kid, he's been talking like this literally since he *could* talk!" Each time the family moved, Richard easily made new friends. Laughed one coach, "It took him forty-five minutes to walk across the school grounds. He talked to everybody!" His teachers and coaches were always scolding him for talking in class, talking in the library, in homeroom, in the hallways, and in the gym during class workouts. His parents confessed that twice they accidentally left him at a city park, because Richard was off talking to other kids and did not get in the car when everyone else did. When the family moved to a new neighborhood in East Los Angeles, Kevin built one of the area's biggest houses. It was very modest, but it had two stories and five bedrooms. Richard made so many friends that on some weekend nights, there would be twenty kids sleeping over. Neighborhood children were such frequent visitors to the Sherman household that they all called Beverly "Auntie."

Stoking the Fire

Sometimes, Branton would get tired of his talkative and popular little brother. Whether they were playing Pokémon or wrestling on the living room floor, Richard kept up a running monologue. Branton, in turn, would counter with taunts. Being three years older, he was bigger and stronger. That tended to put more fire under Richard to compete. The competition between the brothers increased as they got older. Despite how irritating Richard's constant banter was, Branton was always aware that Richard's outgoing personality also had a very generous and kindhearted side. Branton likes to tell the story of when he first started driving and was stopped at a streetlight. A homeless man came up to the car. Richard reached into his pocket and pulled out all of his money, five one-dollar bills. He gave the man four of them.

The Nerd

Although knowing now how his future unfolded, no one today would have thought that in his youth, Richard Sherman was called a "nerd" in school. He got bullied by some students for wanting good grades. Young gang members laughed at him walking through the neighborhood with his stack of books, wearing his glasses. Richard took it in stride, confident that he was heading where he wanted to go. In a recent interview, Sherman said he liked Greek mythology and the Trojan War and read the *Iliad* in school. He laughed and said it wasn't the kind of reading that most people would expect of a football player. His high school counselor said, "His vocabulary was totally different. He didn't talk slang, and the other kids teased him about it." Sherman frequently showed up in the counselor's office wanting to know his grade average and his ranking against other students. In his senior year, Sherman attended leadership seminars and took advanced classes to increase his grade average. The counselor said he was "an extra-credit machine."

Sherman has said that his parents gave him the best advice: you can learn a lot if you go outside your comfort zone. His parents constantly checked to make sure he had done his homework, they talked to his teachers, and they went to open house at school. Besides doing well in school, Sherman also wanted others he cared for to do well in school. If Sherman finished his work before the end of class, he would help his classmates finish theirs. He helped his friends study for tests, including SATs, the college entrance examinations. He told his teammates not to make excuses. If they studied hard, they could become college football prospects, too. The counselor recalls that Sherman's teammates frequently came to his office, asking what they needed to do to get into college. "Because," they would say, "if I don't, Sherm is never going to let me hear the end of it." In the end, Sherman graduated as the class salutatorian, that is, second in his class, with a GPA of 4.2. He averaged higher than a 4.0 (straight A's) by doing a lot of work for extra credit.

A Young Player

Richard's parents stressed academics above all. After academics came sports. From the start, Kevin was involved in sports with his sons. Kevin maintained his early morning shift with the sanitation department so he could be home when the boys got home from school. This gave him time in the afternoons to coach Pop Warner football. When Branton was twelve, he joined a Pop Warner football team, and Richard insisted he was big enough to play, too. He really was not ready physically, but mentally, he was.

Most nights during football season, father and sons could be seen practicing at nearby Ted Watkins Park. In the beginning, Richard was the team mascot, but by age eleven he got his way and started playing with his brother's team. He was so much lighter than the rest of the boys (being two to three years younger), he needed to fill his uniform pockets with bags of sand to pass the required weight minimums. Although he insisted he could play ball, his strength and confidence were not at first apparent. He was actually afraid of being tackled. Kevin got frustrated. One day, he put Richard up against a much bigger player in a tackling drill and told him to "run him over." Richard did and thought he had done well, but it wasn't enough for Kevin. His father told him to do it again. The other player plowed

A teenage Richard Sherman is shown wearing his Dominguez Dons number #4 jersey. His helmet and textbooks are in the foreground.

Richard down. Again, his father told Richard to tackle the player. Three times, Richard was knocked down. Exasperated, Kevin walked over to Richard and picked him up and threw him to the ground, telling him to "do it RIGHT" and "Be a FOOTBALL player!" On the fourth attempt, Richard gave it his all, and tackled the other player to the ground. After that, Richard recalls never being afraid of anything on a football field again.

Branton loved watching his little brother be so competitive. He learned that the way to get Richard to play his best was to goad him. Branton used to make up stories about what opposing players said about Richard. He told Richard that opposing players did not think Richard was any good. Or, he told Richard that HE did not think Richard was any good. "He's going to go for 200 on you today. He's better. He's waaaay better than you!" When Richard heard things like that, he protested, saying they were all wrong, and he was going to prove it. He often boasted that he would get a couple of **picks** [interceptions], recover a couple of fumbles, and score ten touchdowns all in one night. Although it was extreme overconfidence, sometimes Richard managed to come close. When Richard later became a star on his high school football team, his coach agreed, "His motivation is to prove people wrong." The coach said that he always paired Richard against the other team's best wide receiver. Then he would tell Richard that he did not think Richard would be able to cover him because the player was so good, he was going to play college football soon for the University of California or another Division 1 school. That kind of a challenge riled Richard. Often that college-bound player never had a chance to catch even a single pass in any game where Richard covered him.

Before Richard entered Dominguez High School in Compton, he had played basketball, baseball, and football. When he started high school, his brother was a senior. Branton ran on the school's track and field team. Richard, who had never done track and field but was forever his brother's competitor, tried out for the team. Predictably, Richard excelled, and he set school and league records in the 110-meter hurdles, 100-meter sprint, long jump, and triple jump. He was selected as a California All-State first team player and a

USA Today All-American in 2005. Also in 2005, he set a state record and won the state championship with a 50-foot, 8-inch (15.44 m) triple jump.

However, greater athletic accomplishments were on the horizon for Richard. Keith Donerson, coach of the Dominguez High Dons football team, used to lecture his players about commitment and perseverance. Like the many other lessons Richard learned from his parents and teachers, he took the coach's words to heart. From day one on the practice field, Coach Donerson saw Richard's drive and prowess and knew he held enormous promise. Given his strength of character and physical talent, as well as the strong support from his parents, brother, and Coach Donerson, football was going to make Richard Sherman a star.

High School and College Football

lthough he was gangly and not particularly big, Richard Sherman had the athleticism and energy to earn a spot on the Dominguez High School football team, the Dons, in his freshman year. Wearing a Dons' jersey, Sherman began his rise to the NFL. As a freshman, he was five feet nine inches tall (1.75 meters) and weighed 125 pounds (56 kilograms), "dripping wet," as Coach Donerson said. He started as a wide receiver and took on other positions later—**tight end**, kickoff and **punt** returner, and eventually cornerback.

As his success in track and field demonstrated, Sherman could jump, and he had speed. He also had excellent hand-eye coordination and long arms to reach the ball. He was smart, too, and could memorize and react to plays and anticipate other players' moves. Sherman was used as a tight end, blocking when he had to, but always preferring the plays that used him as a receiver. As a freshman receiver, he was frequently outrun and body-slammed by

Opposite: Sherman celebrates with his Stanford teammates after they routed Washington State in 2011 for their fourteenth straight victory.

older players. Sherman was Sherman, though, and he would pop back up after a battering and start heckling his tackler. His coaches were never sure what to do. Sometimes Sherman made them laugh, and other times he angered them. As Coach Donerson said, "Richard never shut up. The way he talks, it's really fast and can be kind of intimidating. We'd go back and forth all the time, but when I tried to muzzle him, he went in the tank." Sherman had too much energy to be silenced. On one hand, it powered him into making exceptional plays, but on the other hand, it got him into trouble.

Sherman caught his first touchdown pass as a fourteen-year-old freshman. At quarterback was Jeron Johnson, who later played defense for the Seattle Seahawks (alongside Sherman). The play exposed Sherman for what he was—a quick and agile receiver. The Dons were behind when Coach Donerson called for a **bubble screen** pass. Sherman was at wide receiver. After the snap, Sherman cut in toward Johnson and caught the pass. The offensive line was playing wide, and Sherman saw the opening he was looking for. Once he got through it, he showed his speed and never looked back.

Coach Donerson believed in running the ball rather than passing. Given that style of play, Sherman had few opportunities as a receiver. Nonetheless, he made the best of it, pulling off some big plays. As Sherman matured, the coach modified his strategy and installed more passing plays. Playing either wide receiver or tight end, Sherman started piling up the numbers. In his junior year, he had 435 receiving yards and scored six touchdowns on only thirteen catches, averaging an impressive 33.4 yards per catch. During that same year, Sherman was also ranked as one of the top high school track and field triple-jumpers in the nation. Track and field gave

Sherman an advantage as a pass receiver; he could do a 10-foot (3 m) standing long jump and had a 37-inch (0.95 m) vertical leap.

In 2004, the Dominguez Dons were establishing themselves as a force to be reckoned with. They made it to the division finals but lost to unbeaten Notre Dame of Sherman Oaks High. That would not happen the following year. In 2005, Sherman's senior year, he was frequently put on defense as cornerback. With his track training, Sherman could run tirelessly and almost fly. Deflecting passes was second nature for him and with his love of the big play, he developed a knack for forcing fumbles and making interceptions. With Jeron Johnson on defense as a middle linebacker, the Dominguez Dons had become formidable. They won thirteen of their fourteen games. In their march toward a championship that year, Sherman gained 859 yards rushing and receiving, plus he gained 157 yards on punt returns, running back three for touchdowns. In a state semifinal matchup against Palos Verdes Peninsula High School, Sherman played cornerback and ran roughshod over its best receiver, shadowing him the entire game and stopping nearly every pass thrown in his direction. The player's name was Nate Carroll, whose father is Pete Carroll, then the coach of the champion University of Southern California Trojans (USC). Coach Carroll was furious, but he did take a good long look at Richard Sherman. The Dons made it to the championship game that year, in large part because of Sherman and Johnson. In that matchup, Richard **sacked** the quarterback and forced a fumble, helping the Dons take the title with a 41–14 blowout of the team that had beaten them the year before, Notre Dame of Sherman Oaks.

The Champ

When Sherman was twelve, he saw a documentary on the life of Muhammad Ali, and it made a lasting impression. Ali was a three-time world heavyweight boxing champion and an Olympic gold medalist. He grew up poor in the segregated South, but through hard work, he achieved greatness and worldwide fame. What set Ali apart from other athletes, besides his prowess, was his forthright speech. When he won his first championship, he boasted, "I am the greatest!" Those words, coming from a black man, angered many whites but instilled pride in African Americans. He was fearless in the boxing ring and outspoken in his opinions on civil rights, segregation, and the Vietnam War.

World champion boxer Muhammad Ali talks to the press after being denied a draft deferment as a conscientious objector.

utting Down an

He was stripped of his titles in 1967, when, as a **conscientious objector** to the Vietnam War, he refused to be drafted into the army. He was sentenced to five years in prison and banned from boxing for three years. Ali stayed out of jail while the courts heard his appeals. The Supreme Court threw out his conviction, and he returned to boxing in 1970. He regained his championship and continued speaking his mind. Ali boasted to his opponents, taunting them with articulate verbal jabs and sometimes poetry. He had been an enormous underdog in his first world championship fight. During the press conference before the fight, he warned his opponent he would "float like a butterfly and sting like a bee." He did. He won. He was "The Champ." Sherman recalls, "Ali knew how to manipulate the world … He created a persona, he was a leader … he knew how to break people down in the ring. I didn't care about boxing, I just wanted to be like Muhammad Ali."

Former USC coach Pete Carroll holds aloft the USC Trojans' Associated Press college football national championship trophy.

Richard Sherman: Shutting Down and Speaking Up

The Recruit

Recruiting eyes were on Sherman early in his junior year. As he transitioned into a triple threat, playing good offense, defense, and special teams, he was an alluring prospect. His first encounter with a recruiter, however, was unofficial. One day, Sherman was called out of class and found Coach Carroll of USC waiting for him in the hallway. The two never left the hallway, just stood there, leaning against lockers and talking football. At one point, Coach Carroll said to Sherman, "You've got the perfect size to be a lock-up corner." After the meeting, Sherman was stunned. He really liked the sound of "lock-up corner" so much that he changed his email address to "lockup2006."

Recruiting started in earnest by his senior year. Several colleges approached him, including the University of Washington, Mississippi State, Nebraska, University of Nevada, University of Colorado, Stanford, and USC. That year, Sherman's classmates voted him as the male student most likely to succeed. Sherman planned on succeeding on two counts—by becoming a professional football player and by getting a first-rate education. He was strong in both—he had a 4.2 GPA, and an SAT score of 1400 (out of 1600). He carried national recruiting ratings of either seventy-four, or three stars out of five. He was determined to smash the stereotype of a "school jock," one who was too cool to care about doing well in school or treating people right. Recruiter Wayne Moses recalls how likeable and popular Sherman was. He said, "You walk across that high school campus with him and you better have some time to do that because you're going to have to stop and talk, people grabbing him and whatnot … He was kind of the mayor."

Sherman attended a regional recruitment camp with other prospects from Southern California. He remembers an exchange he had with another recruit, "One day, a fellow recruit said to me, 'Yo, Uncle Pete come see you yet?'

I was like, 'Uncle who?'

'USC, dawg. Coach Carroll. Uncle Pete.' "

In fact, "Uncle" Pete did come calling again for Sherman, this time officially. However, the coach was left in the physical education department's offices for two and a half hours. Sherman refused to leave an advanced placement (AP) algebra class early. The coach waited. He believed Sherman would be perfect for his style of defense. His USC Trojans were ranked in the top five in the nation. On that day, Sherman had brought only his cleats to school, and Coach Carroll wanted him to run a 40-yard dash on the track. So, Sherman took off his shoes and ran barefoot. He was clocked nowhere near his best time, but Sherman displayed his serious commitment and his adaptability. A full scholarship offer from USC came in soon after.

Sherman continued to consider offers and be interviewed. He made three official recruitment visits—to the University of Washington, Mississippi State, and Stanford. His national recruitment player profile said this:

> Sherman is an athletic playmaker on both sides of the ball as a wide receiver and **safety**. He is tall, lanky, and has long arms. He has a big frame to grow into and he's a long-strider. He moves well, better than his forty time indicates and shows reliable hands …

Sherman was leaning toward Stanford although his family, and in particular Branton, wanted him to go to USC. The Trojans planned to play him as a cornerback, which is the position Sherman preferred. Stanford was projecting Sherman as a wide receiver, not his first choice. For Sherman, however, being accepted into Stanford was a statement he wanted to make about his life. He said, "I'm from Compton, and it's hard for people to understand that you can be an athlete and have high academic standards ... I really wanted people to know that you can go to Stanford from Compton." Sherman visited Stanford, or "The Farm" as it is nicknamed, a few times, each time looking out for the details that could better inform his decision. He wanted to look at the classrooms, dorms, and facilities, and get a feel for what life was like on campus. Many of his football acquaintances wondered why Sherman would choose Stanford, a school with a 5–6 record, versus the Trojans' 12–0 regular season record. That year, the USC Trojans beat the Stanford Cardinal, 51–21, in their **Pac-10** conference game. [NOTE: Stanford's nickname is The Cardinal, as in the color, so the plural form is still Cardinal.] Sherman's response was that he wanted to go somewhere and be a part of change, rather than go to a place that was already winning.

Stanford offered a football scholarship to Sherman, but he had to be accepted academically by the university's admissions office. Sherman had submitted his grades, his SAT test scores, his athletic accomplishments, and a personal essay. In high school, Dominguez students were required to do one hundred hours of community service. Sherman chose to spend all those hours, and more, with the disabled young people his mother worked with. He wrote his essay about his experience. On December 6, 2005, Sherman received a call from Coach Nate Hackett, who told him that he had been admitted to Stanford. Sherman says he was ecstatic. His mother and father ran around the house screaming. He did not commit during that phone call, but he did on January 15, 2006, and signed his letter of intent on February 1, 2006. Sherman has always expressed his tremendous gratitude toward his parents for providing him with the discipline and the support that led him to admission into what he calls "one of the greatest institutions in the world."

The Farm

Kevin and Beverly were elated and very proud of their son. They were also concerned that their son would experience intense and possibly damaging culture shock upon entering Stanford. The university was an elite educational institution that traditionally served students from extremely privileged backgrounds. Percentage-wise, there were few African American or low-income students on campus, and no one at all was from Compton. Even the nickname, The Farm, had its origins in wealth and privilege. The university is sited on the former ranching estate of founders Leland and Jane Stanford.

The coaches at Stanford recognized these concerns and eased Sherman into campus life by enrolling him into summer quarter. It was a good move. Although Sherman did experience some culture shock, he never felt alienated. He said later, "I was with kids from prestigious private schools, and they were drawing comparisons between Plato and Aristotle. A lot went over my head. I had to check out all these books just so I could know what everybody was talking about."

During the 2006 season, Sherman's first, Stanford compiled one of its worst records ever—one win and eleven losses. The bright spot was that Sherman was their leading receiver. He had 34 receptions for 581 yards and tied for the team lead with three touchdowns. That year, Stanford hired a new coach, Jim Harbaugh.

Sherman's alma mater, Stanford University, is one of the nation's premier institutions of higher learning.

Coach Harbaugh was a high-energy person like Sherman. They hit it off well in the beginning. Through the first eight games of the next season, Sherman was again the team's best receiver with 36 catches for 635 yards. During the ninth game, however, Sherman caught only two passes for eleven yards. He lost his self-control and got into a shoving match with a Washington player. He was penalized for unsportsmanlike conduct, and Harbaugh decided to suspend him from the next game. It was then that the two began their falling-out. For the rest of the season, the Cardinal played mostly a running game, and Sherman caught only one pass, for five yards.

Sherman began appealing to assistant coach David Shaw to be allowed to play on the defense. Coach Shaw knew Sherman wanted to play cornerback, but the Cardinal offense relied on him too much to make the change. The coach described Sherman, then a sophomore, as the "one guy on offense who if he touches the ball in the right spot, can score." Sherman proved he could make big plays while surrounded by defenders with a catch on a fourth-and-twenty play in a game against USC. He caught the ball and was tackled immediately just beyond the first down marker on the nine-yard line. The reception set up a Stanford touchdown in a 24–23 win over the Trojans. The Cardinal had come onto the field as 41-point underdogs and left having broken the Trojans' thirty-five-game winning streak.

Clashes of personality continued between Harbaugh and Sherman. In 2008, four games into his junior year, Sherman injured his knee. He applied for a medical redshirt deferment in order to rehabilitate. He was granted redshirt status, meaning he could retain his scholarship and play football for two more years once he recovered from his knee injury. He graduated in four years, so during his fifth year, he studied for a master's degree.

When Sherman returned to the team in 2009, he lobbied Coach Shaw harder for a defensive position. As a pass receiver in a running game, Sherman did not see a lot of action. Being a cornerback could change that. Sherman claimed to have a "defensive player's mentality." Shaw and the Cardinal's secondary coach, Clayton White, agreed. White watched Sherman taunt his **defensive backs** during practice. He believed Sherman not only had the athletic skills to play cornerback but he had "fire." The defensivee coaches refused to try to take "the Compton come out of Sherm." White said, "You want that edge. You want that fire, especially at a school like Stanford, where you don't get many kids who have an edge like Sherm has."

Eventually, Harbaugh relented and allowed Sherman to become a defensive player, but he put Sherman at the bottom of the **depth chart**. That hurt him deeply. As a successful scholarship player, he felt that he deserved more respect. One day, he called his mother and told her that he wanted to transfer out of Stanford. She said to him, "You're going to leave Stanford for some rinky-dink school just because you want to play football and don't get along with some coach? No. You go make it happen." As always, his parents gave him good advice, and Sherman decided he was going to work his way up through the depth chart. He returned to his old ways—pushing himself to his limits and beyond while talking the whole time. He inspired the other defensive players with his energy.

Despite Harbaugh's lack of confidence in his ability to play corner, it turned out that Sherman was especially suited for the position. He was tall, by now six foot three inches (1.9 m), and 195 pounds (88 kg). His excellent catching skills were honed by his years playing as a pass receiver. Above all, he had astounding recall; his memory was nearly photographic. He was an avid student of game film, and on the field he recognized opponents' moves and patterns and reacted quickly. He became masterful at deception, frequently forcing opposing players to make mistakes.

In 2009, his first season back after recovering from his knee injury, Sherman started at cornerback. He proved that he and his defensive coaches had made the right choice. In their conference matchup with USC that season, Sherman was impeccable. With 11:41 left on the clock, the Trojan quarterback threw toward the receiver he was covering. Sherman instantly recalled the play as one he had seen on film, and when the quarterback released the ball, he jumped in front of the receiver, caught the ball, and took it 42 yards down the sideline for a touchdown. In that game, the Cardinal beat the Trojans on their home field, 55–21. Stanford had silenced the normally raucous crowd. Stanford went on to have its first winning season in many years. The next year, Sherman's last, the Stanford Cardinal boasted future NFL professionals such as Andrew Luck at quarterback, Doug Baldwin at wide receiver, and Sherman at cornerback. The team posted a remarkable 12–1 record. It went to the Orange Bowl and beat Virginia Tech, 40–12.

Sherman's conversion to cornerback suited him perfectly. Always athletic, always on the move, he wanted to make plays happen instead of waiting for them. He said, "At receiver, you're limited. If the quarterback has a bad game, you're having a bad game. But at cornerback, no matter what's going on, if your man doesn't catch the ball, you're having a pretty good day. You control your own destiny." Richard Sherman graduated with a Bachelor of Arts degree in communications. He would find that his destiny was not as straightforward as he

Sherman heads for the end zone following an interception against the University of Southern California in a 2009 game played in Los Angeles.

imagined. But armed with talent, brains, and hope, he readied himself for the upcoming NFL draft.

Chapter 3

Reaching the Pros

The Seattle Seahawks had one of the worst defenses in the NFL in 2009. After firing the coach, the team owner, Paul Allen, cofounder of Microsoft, lured Pete Carroll away from USC with the promise of a large contract and a lot of freedom to remake the team. Then, the Seahawks hired a new general manager, John Schneider from Green Bay. The two were a perfect fit. Both had a lot of energy and could think outside the box. Their trading and drafting schemes were different than other teams'. They relied less on game statistics and scouting reports from colleges and more on physical build and athleticism. If those qualities were present, and the player exhibited drive and perseverance, then they believed the prospect was coachable. With the right coaching, good players could become outstanding.

With this attitude, Schneider and Carroll set about rebuilding the team. Many of the players they chose in their first years together, and who were still successful at the end of the 2016 NFL season, were not first-round draft picks. Rather, they were selected in

Opposite: Richard Sherman celebrates a Seattle Seahawks victory over the Arizona Cardinals.

later rounds or signed on as free agents. Anyone who looks at how insightful their strategy is, need look no farther than their having drafted Richard Sherman and several of his star teammates, including Doug Baldwin, Russell Wilson, and Kam Chancellor.

NFL Draft

Sherman had started in all twenty-six games Stanford played in 2009 and 2010. He was instrumental in helping take Stanford's football program from the basement of the Pac-10 Conference to the top. After two years as their leading wide receiver, he spent the last two years as a play-making cornerback. Sherman was confident he would be selected in the 2011 NFL draft in the first round. The draft was broadcast live from New York City. It began on April 28 with the first round and ended April 30 with the fourth through seventh rounds. Sherman and his family rented a hotel room in Las Vegas to watch the events on television. Sherman waited anxiously for a call from the team that drafted him. But on that first day, after the first round was completed, the phone had not rung.

Sherman's college game films showed off his talent. However, many of his statistics did not give an accurate picture of his abilities. The lack of good statistics could be a result of many issues, such as coaching styles, personality clashes, or game strategies. For example, a game largely built on the run will not offer up good statistics for a pass receiver. In many ways, Sherman's less-than-stellar statistics were a result of all of these situations. To make matters worse, Jim Harbaugh failed to endorse Sherman (as well as Doug Baldwin) for the draft.

As a Stanford cornerback and NFL prospect, Sherman performs drills during the 2011 NFL Combine.

In truth, Sherman's **NFL Combine** performance was not remarkable. The NFL Combine invites NFL prospects to undergo a series of tests, such as the bench press, the forty-yard dash, a vertical jump, and an IQ test. Sherman came away from the combine listed as a cornerback, wide receiver, athlete. He ranked 244 out of 750 overall. Published scouting reports gave both positive and negative assessments. CBS Sports said this:

> Positives: Possesses excellent size for the position. Has a lanky, evenly proportioned build with room for additional muscle mass. Good ball skills due to his experience at receiver. Physical. Doesn't back down from the challenge of bigger receivers. May be just scratching the surface of his potential.
>
> Negatives: Questionable speed overall. Has a high **backpedal** and loses a step in his transition, allowing receivers to separate when he misjudges their route, leading to being beaten over the top. Is especially susceptible to smaller, quicker receivers.

NFL.com's write-up said:

> Strengths: Sherman possesses rare height for a corner with enough bulk and speed. Effective when lined up at the line in press man coverage. Uses length well and established sound initial positioning. Flashes the ability to turn and run. Flashes the ability to high-point the football. Willing to help out in run support.
>
> Weaknesses: Sherman does not possess the natural coverage instincts, fluidity or burst to be considered

a future starter. … Has average ball skills but some
upside as a playmaker. Tough against the run but still
developing from a technical standpoint. Sherman is a
Day 3 prospect.

Obviously, Carroll and Schneider saw something others
overlooked. In that draft year, Carroll asked Schneider to find
him a good cornerback. The coach's defensive style was heavy
on cornerback **press coverage**; that is to say, he liked seeing his
defensive backs aggressive, as well as tall, clever, and swift. They saw
all that in Sherman. And more.

Up until that draft year, most teams did not seek out tall corners;
rather, they wanted corners with great speed and turning ability.
They also believed Sherman was too lean to be drafted as a safety,
as players at that position are usually expected to be hard tacklers.
Likely those are the reasons Sherman did not get a phone call until
the third and last day. The Seahawks selected him in the fifth round
as the 154th pick. He was the twenty-fourth cornerback chosen.
Sherman had not expected to be drafted anywhere near that late.
He was furious. Being a fifth-round draft pick, there was a high
likelihood he would get cut from the final roster. He was angry
that, at best, he would be kept on the fifty-three-man roster but be
relegated to playing second or third string. But Sherman, as he had
done before, was determined to prove everyone wrong.

Carroll explained that he had "lost track" of Sherman from his
high school and college days and did not recollect him until he
and Schneider were preparing for the draft. As the coach looked
at Sherman's college game films, however, he remembered how
aggressive and competitive he was. So, when Sherman was still
available in the fifth round, they jumped at the chance to draft him.

Sherman was exactly what Carroll said he was looking for—a tall, athletic, confident, and competitive player. He could run and tackle, and had a desirable **wingspan** of six feet, five-and-a-half inches (1.97 m). (Wingspan is measured from the tip of one middle finger across the chest to the other. Sherman's arms are 32 inches or 0.8 meters long).

Sherman and his family celebrated his becoming a Seattle Seahawk. Carroll called the family and talked to Richard, Kevin, and Beverly (whom he calls "Auntie"). In turn, Beverly gushed over Carroll saying, "We love Petey. He always watched out for Richard." But Sherman, although grateful for his good fortune, walked into the first day of training camp with a self-described big chip on his shoulder.

The Rookie

Pete Carroll said of Sherman, "Richard is about as adept as you can get. He just has extraordinary length, timing, feel and catch-ability … He's a big kid; there are very few kids who play corner like that." But Carroll's task would be to reorient Sherman from a Jim Harbaugh style of play to the style of play the Seahawks were developing. Sherman was in the company of many other new and young players, so he was not alone. However, he needed to move through the learning curve as quickly as possible. Of the ninety players who start training camp, only fifty-three will remain on the roster by the beginning of the NFL season. It came down to the very end of preseason before Sherman learned he had survived the final cut.

On his first day as an official Seahawk, Sherman had a conversation with the defensive coordinator, Gus Bradley. Bradley told him, "A commitment must be made, a plan must be laid, a price must be paid." Sherman not only appreciated the poetry, but he has since muttered it to himself as he practices and plays.

During the first six games of his rookie season, Sherman saw virtually no playing time. He was number four in the depth chart and his stats lay at zero starts, zero passes defensed, and zero interceptions. All the while, Sherman practiced hard, kept up his confidence, and connected with his teammates. But in game seven of the season, everything changed. Season-ending injuries to the starting cornerbacks, Walter Thurmond and Marcus Trufant, put Sherman in the lineup as a starting left cornerback. His first career interception came in that game; he snagged the ball on a deep pass meant for **All-Pro** receiver A.J. Green of the Cincinnati Bengals. With Sherman defending him, Green was able to catch only three passes during that entire matchup. In the next three games, quarterbacks threw to Sherman's side of the field often, expecting to take advantage of a fifth-round rookie, only to see that fewer than half of their passes were caught. In the last four games of the season, quarterbacks realized that the fifth-round rookie was a contender. They passed in his direction far less, and when they did, it still resulted in fewer than half of their passes being caught. Sherman also made three more interceptions, bringing his total to four interceptions in ten games. He had fifty-five tackles in those games, many of them forcing a punt.

By the end of his rookie season, despite starting just ten games, Sherman had been selected by three football organizations as a member of their All-Rookie teams. Voting Sherman onto the team, the Pro Football Writers called his play, "excellent." The Football Outsiders website wrote, "Sherman is a star on the rise according to our game charting numbers, which place him fourth in the league." It is important to point out that Sherman's prominence at this point did not even take into consideration that he played only a little more than half a year.

The Starter

Without a doubt, Carroll, Schneider, and the defensive coaching staff agreed that Sherman had earned a starting position at cornerback. In 2012, Sherman made a name for himself on the field and off. The 2012 season was also the one in which the Seahawks started to make a name for themselves nationally. Their new quarterback, third-round draft pick Russell Wilson, was an unknown who beat out the two veteran quarterbacks on the team. The Seahawks now had a talented young roster on both sides of the field. In 2012, the team would earn its first winning record in five seasons. They would also make the playoffs, playing in the **wild card round** and in the divisional round. They were undefeated at home for the first time in the team's history. Sherman contributed heavily to their success.

Opposite: Sherman intercepts a pass meant for Bengals receiver A.J. Green in his first-ever NFL start at cornerback.

Game Six, against the New England Patriots, catapulted Sherman into the national spotlight. The Patriots had won at least ten games twelve seasons in a row and were led by All-Pro quarterback Tom Brady. The Seahawks, playing before a home crowd of 68,137, were keeping pace somewhat with the Patriots, to the fans' thunderous delight. Sherman had several opportunities to show off his ball-handling skills. One came in the third quarter with the Patriots leading, 20–10. Lined up as a **slot** cornerback (not his preferred position), he was in press coverage against the speedy Deion Branch. When the ball was snapped, Branch stepped quickly to his right, and with him, followed Sherman. They both turned and went deep down the field. Brady lobbed a long, high pass, but it was Sherman, being uncommonly tall for a cornerback, who came down with the ball for an interception. It was the first pass Brady had had intercepted in 179 attempts. In that same game, strong safety Earl Thomas intercepted Brady again, this time in the end zone. During a television commercial break, Brady and Thomas had a little back-and-forth discussion over Thomas's and Sherman's interceptions. Brady mocked them by saying, "Who are you guys? Come and see me after we win." His taunts sent the Seahawks into overdrive in the fourth quarter, and they upset the Patriots, 24–23. After the game, a photograph was taken of Richard coming up to talk to Brady. Sherman's dreadlocks were flying and Brady was looking down, scowling. Sherman posted that image on Twitter, superimposing on the photo the words "U mad, Bro?" He took the post down soon after, but not before it circulated widely and became an internet **meme**, a popular T-shirt, and a poster.

Week eight against the Detroit Lions provided another chance for Sherman to be in the limelight. The Detroit Lions' massive

Sherman posted this photo with Patriots quarterback Tom Brady on social media with the caption, "U mad, Bro?"

Reaching the Pros

First Team All-Pro wide receiver, Calvin Johnson, was Sherman's responsibility. At six feet five inches, Johnson was not an average receiver. As a matter of fact, teammates and fans called him "Megatron." In the week prior to the game, Sherman changed his Twitter name to "Optimus Prime," causing a stir. (For those who may not know anything about Transformers comics, Optimus Prime is the leader of the good guys, the Autobots, and Megatron is the leader of the bad guys, the Decepticons.) Opponents of Sherman's style called him out for personally baiting Johnson. Sherman responded that it was all fun and games. Peter Cullen, the actor who provides the voice of Optimus Prime, must have agreed with Sherman. He called Sherman before the game, using Optimum Prime's voice to say, "One shall stand, one shall fall. Wish you the best. Roll out!" Though the Seahawks did not come away with a win, Sherman held Johnson to only three catches for 46 yards.

In a Veteran's Day game, the Seahawks overtook the New York Jets, 28–7. Sherman earned NFL defensive player of the week in that game. On a third-down-and-goal play, Sherman tricked the quarterback, Mark Sanchez, to throw across the field. Sherman moved in for the interception, his fourth so far that year. He also made the first quarterback sack of his career on a **blitz** from the Seattle 32-yard line. The sack caused a fumble that the Seahawks recovered.

Getting On a Roll

In week fourteen, the Seahawks had a rematch with the Arizona Cardinals. The first time the teams met, the Cardinals beat the Seahawks, 20–16. This second game was not close by any measure. The Cardinals committed eight **turnovers**. Sherman had two interceptions, one of which he returned 19 yards for a touchdown. He also had three tackles and a fumble recovery. The result was the largest margin of victory in a shutout in the nearly fifty-year history of the Seattle Seahawks, 58–0.

For the following game the Seahawks traveled to Toronto, Ontario, to play the Buffalo Bills. At the time, the Seahawks were rated the number three defense in the NFL, propelled, many say, by Sherman's inspiring energy. Defensive lineman and teammate Byron Maxwell said, "You need different dynamics in a group, and that's what Richard Sherman provides. He's that passion. He's that sparkplug." The Seahawks won that game, 50–17. The Seahawks were the first team since 1950 to score fifty or more points in consecutive games.

In week sixteen of the regular season, the Seahawks went up against the San Francisco 49ers, now coached by Harbaugh, the former coach at Stanford. Although the Seahawks had already clinched a wild card spot in the playoffs, playing the 49ers always brought out the fire in Sherman. In this game, he let fly. He had five tackles and intercepted quarterback Colin Kaepernick. He also recovered a blocked 49ers' field goal attempt and ran 90 yards for a touchdown. The final score was 42–13. Those were the most points scored against the 49ers since Harbaugh took over as coach.

In the last three games, the Seahawks had outscored their opponents, 150–30. In the next and final game of the regular season, the Seahawks beat the St. Louis Rams by a more modest margin of 20–13. On one play, Sherman was lined up across from a bunched group of three receivers, and it was his responsibility to figure out which one to cover. Sam Bradford, the Rams' quarterback, was trying to overwhelm Sherman with multiple possible routes. However, Sherman had studied Bradford on film and deduced that he would throw to the shorter, faster, slot receiver. Sherman edged closer to the slot receiver as they ran downfield. As if on cue, Sherman cut in front of the receiver and intercepted the ball. After that victory at home, the Seahawks had a record of 11–5, had a five-game winning streak, and were headed for the 2012 playoffs as a wildcard team (they finished second in the NFC West division). They had given up a league-low average of 15.3 points per game.

Seattle fans went wild over their revived team, studded with late-round and undrafted players who became stars. The first playoff game, a wildcard game against the Washington Redskins, was on the road. In the first half, the Seahawks fell behind 14–0, but rallied to win, 24–14. It was their first road playoff victory since 1983. Of course, Sherman cannot seem to avoid attracting attention in big games, especially those with high stakes. After winning the game, he and Washington **Pro Bowler** Trent Williams had a heated argument on the sidelines. During the exchange, Sherman goaded Williams and, in front of the television cameras, Williams slapped Sherman in the face. The next day, Williams released a statement:

> I want to take this opportunity to apologize for my actions that took place following tonight's game. It was a hard-fought game between two great teams, and I let my emotions get the best of me. To Richard Sherman, the Seahawks, my teammates, and all the fans … I am truly sorry. I feel as though I've taken many strides to be a better person this season and this is not how I wanted it to end. And for that, I apologize for my actions.

Opposite: Sherman and Washington offensive tackle Trent Williams spar verbally. Williams slapped Sherman in the exchange and apologized later.

Players and fans chimed in on Twitter on both sides of the fence. One side believed that Sherman deserved to be slapped for being mouthy, while others liked Sherman's spunk backed up with first-class talent.

In the division playoff, the Seahawks lost to the Atlanta Falcons in the last few seconds of the game. After the loss, sad and disappointed, the team studied the game film. Carroll and the team agreed that they did not want to feel so melancholy again. They were going forward, "Our future is bright," said defensive end Red Bryant.

Smarts

The team and its fans knew the future was bright for many reasons, in no small part due to what Richard Sherman brought to the game. Quarterback Russell Wilson had been exceptionally smart in leading the offense, and Sherman had cleverly turned the Seahawks' defensive secondary into one of the most feared in the league. Safety Earl Thomas called him a genius. Sherman has a near-photographic memory. Thomas said that once when Sherman was visiting his home and asked for his home network Wi-Fi password, Sherman instantly memorized an eighteen letter-and-number hodgepodge.

Beyond being a superb athlete, Sherman is a devoted student of the game. He excels at preparation. His brilliance is most apparent when he studies film. He has been an avid game film reviewer since his days as a Dominguez Don. During the NFL season, when he is not on the field or in practice, Sherman is likely camped out with his iPad, studying film. He constantly asks questions and madly scribbles notes. "Some dudes play with pure athleticism," says Sherman, "I'm not one of those guys."

Sherman not only knows the playbook, he knows the rulebook.

For example, in a game against the Buffalo Bills in 2016, he showed his command of the rules, and with that knowledge helped prevent the Bills from winning in the last minute. As Bills quarterback Tyrod Taylor swung out of the **pocket** looking for a receiver in the end zone, Sherman knew that it would then be legal for him to make contact with the receiver he was covering. While many thought knocking down the unsuspecting receiver deserved a penalty flag, his play was instead absolutely legal. Thanks to Sherman and the defense, the Seahawks kept their lead and won the game. As Carroll has said, "He's got a great mind. He's bright, he's sharp. He's got wit, he's got creativity to him, which is really what his game is like as well."

Before any snap, Sherman eyes the movements around the line of scrimmage intently. Key to Sherman's expertise is his ability to bait quarterbacks into throwing passes his way. His ability at being both a quick study and tirelessly fast make him one of the best **shutdown cornerbacks** in the league. Sportswriters praise Sherman's shrewdness. From Fox Sports: "Seattle Seahawks cornerback Richard Sherman is one of the smartest players on the field at just about any given moment." From CBS Sports: "Richard Sherman is scary smart." Off the field, Sherman entertains reporters with unconventional news conferences and spirited pregame rants. He is a genius for convincing future opponents that they have trouble ahead. He gets inside their heads, not unlike Muhammad Ali.

All for One, One for All

Pete Carroll is a masterful strategist and doesn't make his players follow a lot of regulations. His motto is "compete, compete, compete." Yet the environment he creates for the team in the locker

A Battle of Wills

There have been many talented cornerbacks in the game, such as Darrelle Revis, who Sherman challenged for supremacy. However, it is often said that Sherman's biggest football rival is his former college coach, Jim Harbaugh. Sherman was recruited to Stanford by a coach who knew he was getting a smart, athletic, and very vocal student athlete. A year later, that coach was gone, replaced by Harbaugh. Not very far into their relationship, Sherman and Harbaugh started to clash. Harbaugh could not accept Sherman's intense and outspoken ways. About Harbaugh, Doug

Coach Jim Harbaugh walks on the sidelines during a Stanford game. Richard Sherman is wearing the number 9 jersey.

Baldwin said, "I'd say he's more of a disciplinarian type of coach. He likes to be in control of things."

Eventually, Harbaugh let Sherman play cornerback, but he dropped him in the depth chart and commented, "Don't know if he'll be able to beat anybody out over there or not." One of Coach Harbaugh's assistant coaches told Sherman, "You may never play football again, but your chances will be enhanced if you keep your mouth closed."

During a Stanford vs. USC game, Harbaugh called for a two-point conversion. It came during a 55–21 rout of USC, and it spurred the Trojans coach Pete Carroll to ask, "What's your deal?" For this and other perceived actions by Harbaugh, Sherman has called him a bully. Later, during an NFL game between the Seahawks and Harbaugh's 49ers, the 49ers were behind by a score of 42–13. Harbaugh complained that the Seahawks were being too physical. Sherman wanted vengeance and urged Carroll to keep running up the score. That game happened to be played on Harbaugh's birthday, and Sherman said he had a present for him, "a ninety-yard touchdown."

The Seahawks' secondary, known as the Legion of Boom, links arms after a win before giving interviews to the press.

room and on the field is supportive and enthusiastic. He plays rap and hip-hop music during practice, and there is a basketball hoop in the meeting room, creating an environment that is a far cry from what most other teams experience. Carroll has said he believes in letting players be themselves, to a degree. Admittedly, Sherman tests that boundary often, but so far, the Seahawks recognize that Sherman's swagger and constant chatter and trash-talk are fuel for his stellar performances. When Sherman first learned he was coming to Seattle, his friends in California teased him that he was headed for "South Alaska," and that nobody would ever care about the Seahawks. Many people told him that the NFL was all business, and that people were going to reject him for his brash and high-spirited style. However, the Seahawks players formed solid bonds. Their team culture is one in which people are glad for another's success. They are all competitors, but they are not afraid to help anyone else improve. As Sherman explained, "I think that the teams that are the most successful are the teams that have fun doing what they're doing. It just goes against the grain of what the perception is of what football is supposed to be. It's not supposed to be fun, it's supposed to be hard and rigorous, and you fight for your wins. Here, we have a fun time practicing, we have a fun time in our meetings, and that ultimately leads to us having a fun time out there on the field game day—which I think contributes to our success."

Chapter 4

Roll On!

By 2013, Pete Carroll, his coaching staff, and the team's strong, smart, young players had become a dominant force in the NFL. When training camp began that season, predictions came in across the board that the NFC winner and, likely, the next Super Bowl champion, would come from the highly competitive NFC West, whose teams include the Seahawks, the San Francisco 49ers, the Arizona Cardinals, and the Los Angeles Rams. Fans and the sports world were looking forward to some fiery and confrontational division match-ups. They got what they were asking for.

Many in the sports world were mystified how a team could develop so fast, and with so many rookie and late-round draft picks and free-agent players. Adding to the mystery was how Carroll had done it. Although he had run a successful program at USC, he had also had two previous short and not-very-productive stints as an NFL head coach. Additionally, he had been out of the pro game for eleven years. Gus Bradley, his Seahawks defensive coordinator, also did not

Opposite: Richard Sherman celebrates after an interception in a road game against the New York Giants in 2013.

have a long or particularly noteworthy history in the NFL. Regardless, Carroll turned the Seahawks' offense into a high-scoring unit and by the end of the season, had molded the Seahawks' defense into the best in the league. With second-year quarterback Russell Wilson at the helm of the offense, and Sherman the de facto leader of the defense, the Seahawks ended the year with a 13–3 record. Before Carroll came on board in 2008, Seattle had a record of 4–12. The Seahawks continued having losing seasons until 2012 (although they did win the division title in 2010 with a record of 7–9), where they jumped to 11–5. All the games that they lost in 2012 and 2013 were decided by seven points, or one touchdown, or less.

As the Seahawks rolled through the 2013 season, winning eleven of their first twelve games, Sherman became not only the face of the Seahawks, but the voice. Articulate and entertaining in interviews, he has written pieces for *Sports Illustrated,* appears regularly in the *Monday Morning Quarterback* column, and regularly writes multimedia columns for *The Players' Tribune* titled "Tuesdays with Richard on Thursdays." His topics are diverse, and he shows not only his intellect and emotion, but his leadership qualities.

The Legion of Boom

The Legion of Boom is a testament to the Seahawks' intense bond. It is the nickname, coined by safety Kam Chancellor, to describe the heart of the Seahawks' secondary, originally made up of cornerbacks Richard Sherman and Byron Maxwell (who replaced Brandon Browner, who signed with the Patriots) and safeties Earl Thomas and himself. The nickname is a takeoff on the cartoon characters called the Legion of Doom. The group first bonded by playing pickup basketball. Chancellor was very impressed with Sherman

The Seahawks' secondary enjoys the Super Bowl victory parade in Seattle.

for his brash, trash-talking ways. "We were on defense, and he's just talking trash to whoever came down court. That was his first mentality. After we played basketball, I could see how he just trash-talked and backed that up with competitiveness." Earl Thomas was the only first-round draft pick in this powerhouse of Pro Bowl players—Sherman and Chancellor were selected in the fifth round, and Maxwell in the sixth. Brandon Browner was recruited from the Canadian Football League (CFL). Since the beginning, the Legion of Boom has been a true brotherhood. They say "I love you" before every game, and they mean it. In 2011, Sherman was not selected for the Pro Bowl in his short rookie year. Other members of the defense were. As an example of their bond, they took Sherman with them to Hawaii for the game. In 2014, *Time* magazine included Sherman as one of the one hundred most influential people for the year. His photograph for the cover included the other members of the Seahawks' secondary, as Sherman refused to be photographed without them.

Defense, Sherman Style

Quarterbacks and receivers try their best to avoid the dangerous shoals around "Sherman Island." When Sherman lines up wide with a receiver on his "island," he is rarely outplayed. His speed and intuition take over even as the receiver gets the first move and knows where the ball is headed. Commonly, the best cornerback is assigned to cover the opponent's best receiver, and Sherman has made spectacular plays in those conditions. Man-to-man coverage is one of the most difficult assignments on the field. Sherman also shows his strength in the Seahawks' **zone defense**, in which he patrols half the field.

Cornerback is one of the most physically draining positions. Receivers get rotated in and out of the lineup throughout the game, but starting cornerbacks do not. With every snap, the cornerback tracks his man and runs in coverage or tries to make a tackle.

"As corners, we never leave the game," explains Sherman, "That's part of the challenge. It's also all part of the chess match. When you get to the fourth quarter, nobody is 100 percent. That's when ballers ball. That's when stars shine. When it comes to playing cornerback, you're on an island out there. It doesn't matter if you're hurt or you're tired, if there's a minus-25-degree wind chill [−31°Celsius] or if the

NFC championship is on the line. At the end of the day, the only thing that matters is … Can you make a play?"

Yes, he can.

As dynamic and innovative as the Super Bowl-bound Seahawks were in 2013, they still used a basic **4-3 alignment** on defense (four linemen, three linebackers). Given the versatility of the Seahawks' secondary, it proved successful. The Seahawks are aggressive in their pass defense and a good part of their line of attack is cerebral. The defensive units, and Sherman almost fanatically, study game films to gain an edge on their opponents.

"If you don't have the mental aspect of the game down, that's one advantage opponents have on you," Sherman says. "Because you know, everybody has the physical attributes at this level—everybody can run fast, jump high, do everything you need to do to be successful. But studying film for hours and hours, and watching receivers, and watching splits, and watching second down, third down, first down, **red zone,** everything, that gives you a different kind of strategic advantage. Because, when it's third and five, and you've watched every third and five they've had for the last four or five games, you know which route combinations they like out of which formations. And when they show you the formations you want to see, it makes it very easy to stop them."

Sherman is one of the most prepared players in the league. He produced a video for the NFL that broke down game film and described the complex details of the cornerback position. In one part of the video, he talks about how much he practices tipping the ball into the hands of his teammates for interceptions. That skill would bring him fame, fortune, and notoriety later in the 2013 season.

Super Season

Sherman came into the 2013 season already changing how the NFL looks at cornerbacks. He proved he could be dominant with his body type. He is not the fastest corner in the league, but he is aggressive and physical. By playing press coverage and legally pushing receivers at the line of scrimmage, he forces receivers to stutter just long enough to throw off their timing with the quarterback, and sometimes, redirects their routes. "A lot of corners will back up and give a receiver room to move," Sherman explains. "Seahawks corners don't back up. We don't give any room. We stay in their face all day long."

The Seahawks' pass defense uses more press coverage than other teams. Sherman says that he uses it about fifty times a game, where most teams may on only three or four plays. Meanwhile he reads quarterbacks well and generally can deduce where they plan to throw the ball. His technique led to twenty interceptions in just his first two and a half seasons.

Sherman and the Legion of Boom allowed the fewest passing yards in the 2013 season—an average of just 175.6 yards per game. In 2013, they grabbed a league-leading 28 interceptions and returned those interceptions for 385 yards; 125 of those yards were Sherman's. The Legion of Boom jokingly calls its part of the field the "No Fly Zone." Sherman, Chancellor, and Thomas were named to the Pro Bowl as well as All-Pro that season.

With Sherman chanting, "We're getting somewhere. We're getting somewhere," the Seahawks started the 2013 season with the Super Bowl on their radar. After winning their first game, the second was a matchup with their division rivals, the 49ers. It was a sloppy

Sherman loses a shoe after intercepting a pass against Houston in 2013 but still runs for a game-tying touchdown.

Roll On!

game on many counts, and included a break to allow a lightning storm to pass through. The field was muddy, and quarterbacks Wilson and Kaepernick had bad days. The Seahawk defense held the 49ers to just three points in what was ultimately a 29–3 victory. It was also responsible for generating most of the scoring. They caused a safety to give the Seahawks a 2–0 lead early in the second quarter, and later, both Kam Chancellor and Earl Thomas made interceptions that led to touchdown runs by Marshawn Lynch. But for most of the game, Sherman was quiet. He had asked to play in one-on-one coverage with wide receiver Anquan Boldin, who had scorched Green Bay the week prior. With Sherman shadowing Boldin, Kaepernick had no intention of passing to him. Sherman and Boldin spent most of the game together on Sherman Island. But never one to go without notice, Sherman intercepted a pass in the end zone in the fourth quarter. Excited for his first interception of the season, he celebrated by dancing on the sidelines with the cheerleading squad.

The Seahawks began the 2013 season with four straight wins for the first time in team history. In the fourth game, against the Houston Texans, the Seahawks trailed by 17 points, 20–3, at halftime. The Seahawks had come into the game ranked number one on defense. Although the offense had rallied in the third quarter, Seattle was still down by a touchdown with three minutes remaining in the game. The Texans had the ball on a third down. Sherman and the rest of the secondary had studied game film all week and believed that in this situation, the quarterback, Matt Schaub, would pass. So, as they had predicted and practiced on Friday, they recognized the upcoming play. Thomas and Chancellor disguised their intentions, tricking Schaub into throwing a short pass over to his slot receiver, Owen Daniels. The secondary's deception worked and cleared the way for Sherman to intercept the ball. After he made the catch, Sherman had one of his shoes come off. Unperturbed, he ran downfield for 58 yards and a touchdown. The defense had tied the game, and Steven Hauschka kicked a field goal for the 23–20 win in overtime. "That game was all about grit," said coach Carroll.

"Best Corner in the Game"

The Seahawks qualified for the 2013 postseason as the number one seed in the NFC, with a bye and **home field advantage**. In their first playoff game, against the New Orleans Saints, the weather could not have been more miserable in Seattle. There were gale-force winds and driving rain. It was almost impossible to throw a football against the wind, and both teams had to rely on the run and on defense. In the first half, the New Orleans Saints quarterback, Drew Brees, was not able to complete a single pass beyond the line of scrimmage, compliments of the Seattle secondary. Brees heated up in the fourth quarter but the Seahawks put held on to beat the Saints, 23–15.

The next week, in the NFC Championship game in Seattle, Sherman would be on top of his game, for better and for worse. The game pitted two young quarterbacks against each other for the third time that season—Kaepernick of the 49ers and Wilson of the Seahawks. The teams had split games, each winning once against the other, during the regular season. It was a game for the ages, hard-fought and brutal. Fueling the animosity was not only the chance to play in a Super Bowl, but the simmering feud between Carroll, Sherman, and Baldwin of the Seahawks and Harbaugh and the rival 49ers.

Sherman deflects a pass meant for Michael Crabtree, sealing the Seahawks' NFC championship title and a trip to the Super Bowl.

The game was a back-and-forth battle. In the fourth quarter, the Seattle defense forced three turnovers. The last turnover is part of NFL history. During the game, for the most part, Sherman covered Michael Crabtree, a wide receiver for the 49ers. A longstanding and intense feud existed between Sherman and Crabtree, the most recent incident being a snipe by Crabtree toward Sherman at a charity event. In any case, Kaepernick avoided targeting Crabtree because Sherman was assigned to him in one-on-one coverage. However, with thirty seconds left in the game and San Francisco trailing by six points, the 49ers had reached the Seahawks' 18-yard line. When Kaepernick saw Crabtree in the end zone, he could not resist throwing to him. It would mean the Super Bowl for the 49ers, and Crabtree appeared wide open. However, Sherman was there and with his height, he leapt as Crabtree leapt. Falling backward toward the rear of the end zone, Sherman kept his feet in bounds. As in practice, he swiped at the ball, batting it toward teammate Malcolm Smith, who made the interception with twenty-two seconds left in the game. It was a stunning play by Sherman, and it propelled the Seahawks into the Super Bowl for the first time since their only previous appearance in 2005.

Emotion on everyone's part was soaring. CenturyLink Field was a madhouse. The Seahawks fans, who call themselves the Twelfth Man, stomped, jumped, and screamed so loudly that they registered a magnitude 2.0 earthquake in downtown Seattle. Geologists have since installed permanent earthquake monitors in the stadium.

The Aftermath

It was during the postgame celebration when Sherman gave a sideline interview that would provoke controversy throughout the

Quotes by Richard Sherman

Here are some of the best quotes uttered or posted by Richard Sherman.

"Got off my flight to this hilarious convo. So I have 8 picks, 3 ff [forced fumbles] and a sack. My season stats looking like Revis's career stats."

—During a Twitter feud on February 20, 2013, with then Tampa Bay cornerback Darrelle Revis

"I'm intelligent enough and capable enough to understand that you are an ignorant, pompous, egotistical cretin. I'm going to crush you on here because I'm tired of hearing about it."

—To host Skip Bayless on ESPN's *Fresh Take* program, March 7, 2013

"I'm not a villain. I'm just a very rude football player from time to time."

—At a press conference on January 22, 2014, prior to the Super Bowl

"I saw a hockey game where they didn't even play hockey. And I'm a thug? I know some thugs, and they know I'm the farthest thing from a thug."

—At the same press conference on January 22, 2014, prior to the Super Bowl

"You're not on scholarship for school, and it sounds crazy when a student-athlete says that, but that's— those are the things coaches tell them every day: 'You're not on scholarship for school.'"

> —At a press conference on January 30, 2015, prior to playing in his second Super Bowl

"What challenge?"

> —when asked about the "challenge" of playing against Atlanta Falcons wide receiver Roddy White in a story posted by NBC Sports on November 8, 2013

sports world. It became a bigger story than the upcoming Super Bowl. When the teams were coming off the field, people could see Crabtree and Sherman having words and gesturing. When Sherman went to shake Crabtree's hand to say "good game," it was not taken well, and Crabtree shoved Sherman. Right after that, Sherman stepped onto the sidelines, full of adrenaline from the biggest play of his career, and was caught by Fox News and ESPN sports reporters for an interview. Sherman was agitated by the encounter with Crabtree. When reporter Erin Andrews asked about tipping the ball and saving the game, he went off on a rant, claiming that he was the best cornerback in the league, and disparaging Crabtree by calling him a sorry and mediocre receiver. Sports interviews are generally loaded with platitudes and clichés. What reporters got this time was anything but. Reporters, pundits, and fans instantly chimed in online. Media members from newspapers, magazines, television, radio, the blogosphere, and social media could not resist the subject of Richard Sherman. Few doubted his claim that he was the best cornerback in the league; he had certainly proved it by his last play, but many were turned off by his rant. During the postgame news conference, Sherman was calm and charming, his heat-of-the-moment outburst behind him. Yet, the story was not over.

Plenty of taunts are bandied about on the field among players, but Sherman's interview brought up serious discussions about social issues. Most of the immediate reactions were negative and nasty. People called Sherman classless, ignorant, a jerk, a thug, and countless unprintable racist epithets. In commenting about the bad blood between him and Crabtree, Sherman said, "I know if I went up to Larry Fitzgerald in that situation, he'd have shaken my hand. It's about respect." Sherman suggested that "thug" had become society's

San Francisco 49ers wide receiver Michael Crabtree slaps Sherman away after the Seahawks' win in the NFC championship game.

Roll On!

Richard Sherman speaks out to Erin Andrews in his controversial post-NFC championship game interview.

code for the "N-word," and it seemed clear he had a case. Several days later, Sherman agreed to an interview with CNN. He was "well spoken, eloquent, and articulate," according to reports afterward. For many, those words symbolized society's endemic racism—why were people surprised that a black man, a black athlete, was "eloquent?" Is it unimaginable considering that Sherman graduated with a 3.9 GPA in communications from Stanford? If not, then why would his "eloquence" be a surprise?

Sherman later extended an apology to Crabtree. However, he wrote in his *Sports Illustrated* column about the racial attacks he experienced: "To those who would call me a thug or worse because I show passion on a football field—don't judge a person's character by

Wowed in Seattle

Writers on the Seahawks vs. the 49ers:

Did you see the two most physical teams in football beat each other half to death? Did you see all the brutal hits? Did you see all the players who couldn't get up after the play? Did you see all those guys who had to be helped off the field? ... That was the kind of game it was. Rough and angry and so violent that at times it was hard to watch. Richard Sherman made the big play Sunday. His team is going to the Super Bowl. More important, he survived the carnage. It seems to me that the only proper response to surviving something like that is to holler like a crazy person. —Forbes magazine

Sherman never stopped talking this year, and the Seahawks have backed it up with an incredible season. The Seattle defensive unit closed in style. San Francisco's final four drives: three-and-out, sack-fumble, interception, interception. On the biggest stage and through the biggest plays imaginable, Sherman and the Seahawks' defense made sure that everyone keeps talking about them for the next two weeks. —NFL.com

On the last meaningful play of a very meaningful game, Seahawk cornerback Richard Sherman made a play that perhaps no other human on the planet could have made, pirouetting in mid-air to swat away what seemed a sure game-winning touchdown. Game over. Seahawks win, 23–17, and advance to play the Denver Broncos in the Super Bowl February 2. There was wholesale carnage, however, before that moment of athletic grace. —Mark Sappenfield, Christian Science Monitor

what they do between the lines. Judge a man by what he does off the field, what he does for his community, what he does for his family."

Super Bowls

The media stayed focused on Sherman in the two weeks leading up to the Super Bowl. The Seahawks, with the best defense in the league, came into the game as two-point underdogs to the Denver Broncos, led by future Hall of Fame quarterback Peyton Manning. For anyone but a Seattle Seahawks fan, it was one of the worst Super Bowls of all time. The Seahawks scored a safety against the Broncos on the opening play from scrimmage and went on to produce the third biggest rout in Super Bowl history, a 43–8 thrashing of the Broncos. The Seahawks returned home to see all of Seattle lit up in blue and green (the team colors), including the iconic Space Needle.

Seattle Seahawks fans turned out in full force to celebrate the Seahawks' Super Bowl victory.

Coach Carroll hugs Sherman as he comes off the field after a big play during the Super Bowl.

More than a half-million fans showed up for the victory parade through downtown.

Sherman had another phenomenal season in 2014, albeit one in which fewer passes came his way, which is an indication of his dominance. In the 2014 NFC conference playoff game with Green Bay, Sherman injured his arm in the first quarter. He held his arm to his side like a "wounded bird" and winced throughout the game. He stayed in, knowing that quarterback Aaron Rogers would still not target him, restricting the game effectively to just half the field. Regardless of the pain, Sherman made an interception in the end zone, validating for many that he was the best corner in the game, even with just one arm. The Seahawks won the NFC championship and returned to the Super Bowl that year, where they lost to the New England Patriots on a goal-line interception in the final minute. When the Patriots quarterback, Tom Brady, took a knee on the last play to run out the clock, Sherman was the first to come up to him, holding out his hand in congratulations.

Opposite: Richard Sherman shakes Tom Brady's hand after the Patriots' dramatic victory in the Super Bowl.

Chapter 5

The Real Richard Sherman

With his sensational tipped-pass play in the 2013 NFC championship game, Richard Sherman had sent his team to the Super Bowl. At the same time, he lit up the media with his "I am the best corner in the game" declaration. The stir took a while to settle down, but as reporters and others followed the story and looked closer into Sherman's background, they discovered that what the outstanding All-Pro does off the field is likewise outstanding.

His postgame rant may have been unsportsmanlike, but it was misleading about his true character. The real Richard Sherman is a generous man and a wholehearted advocate for disadvantaged youth. Knowing this, then–First Lady Michele Obama asked Sherman to participate in a video promoting Let's Move, her national program to encourage children to eat healthier foods. In the video, Sherman and teammates Earl Thomas and Byron Maxwell cooked up a meal of fish cakes and vegetables. The first

Opposite: Mo'ne Davis and Lindsey Vonn present Sherman with the 2014 ESPY award.

Sherman and then-First Lady Michelle Obama joke on the set of a video for the Let's Move program that encouraged children to eat healthier.

lady and Sherman spoofed on his famous rant. She played the role of interviewer, while Sherman yelled, "We the best chefs in the game!"

Sherman does much more than encourage kids to eat right. His concern for others was first apparent in school, when he helped his high school teammates study for exams and pass in their homework. After leaving for Stanford, Sherman kept his eyes on his former friends and teammates in Compton. He called them, texted them, and did his best to shepherd them through school. He helped many apply for college, scholarships, and financial aid. One of his closest friends, Marcus "Scooby" Peters, was set to enter Cal State. Sherman had helped him get all his paperwork in to the school. But in May 2007, Scooby and a friend were walking down a street in Long

Beach and were shot by two men. Scooby did not survive. Alone, at Stanford, Sherman was distraught but even more determined to help others from the inner city take steps to move on. Explaining his feelings in an essay, he wrote, "I can't change who I grew up with, but what I can do is try to educate them on the right way of doing things, help them when they need it, and try to keep them out of trouble." Sherman also helped his brother get out of trouble. After Branton attended Boise State, he returned to Los Angeles and got involved with selling drugs and wound up in jail. When Sherman was drafted, he told Branton to come up to Seattle and "work hard and make things happen." Branton is now a successful businessman.

At Stanford, Sherman was acutely aware of his economically disadvantaged background. "In Compton," said Sherman, "walking meant being visible, and being visible meant being in danger from a gang-fueled siege of constant random violence. When I got here [Stanford], I could walk anywhere and wear anything. Oh, my God, if they only knew back home." Yet his recently acquired wealthy and privileged surroundings did not intimidate him. He did not turn away from his past. He was proud of his accomplishments and still believed he had something to offer others. Coach Shaw remembers asking the football team to volunteer at "Football Camp for the Stars," an event for athletes with Down syndrome. Shaw said Sherman was the first to raise his hand, remarking, "He was there at the beginning, and he stayed past the end. He is the farthest thing from a thug you can imagine. Thugs don't volunteer to help out at the Special Olympics."

Sherman spends several weeks each year visiting elementary and high schools in low-income neighborhoods, mostly in the Seattle area and in Los Angeles. The day after Sherman's infamous interview

Sherman entertains children at a charity event for Children Mending Hearts, an organization that provides activities for at-risk children.

with Erin Andrews, he visited a local school and encouraged students to give themselves goals and to make plans to achieve them. After each of his assemblies, Sherman meets with students who are at risk for failing or dropping out of school. He asks them to sign a pledge agreeing to improve their grades, stay in school, and be good citizens. For that, Sherman gives them a backpack full of school supplies and the promise that he will be there for them, if they hold up their side of the deal to do well.

Sherman tells the students that there are plenty of people from Compton and similar neighborhoods who have become successful. He tells them not to be victims of stereotypes and reminds them that even if they feel trapped or hopeless, he is living proof that success can happen by working hard and setting goals. When the students whom Sherman mentors need help, he is always there. A former Dominguez football player said, "If I need something, I can ask him … It's never a problem. It's never 'No' with him. It's not even in his vocabulary." In return, Sherman emphasizes his desire to be supportive, "They know I'm tangible, they know I'm here. Any chance I can get to give back—whether it be cleats, helmets, or just someone to speak to—anything I can do to help I try to get done. Because without this place [Compton], I don't think I'd be the man or the player I am today." Donerson says he has always spoken about Sherman's drive and responsible behavior to his students, and because Sherman comes back and visits Compton, it makes him a powerful reality for them and not just a story.

Sherman attributes his urge to give back to the support and teaching he received from his parents. After one school visit, Sherman said:

I can only hope that the students received my message that day. I wanted to let them know that they will face challenges at some point in life, but if they use their intelligence and intuition, they can get past these problems and come out a better person. If you put in the work, put in the time, put in the effort, you're going to reap the benefits.

Some of these kids aren't as fortunate though. That's why I do these visits. I want them to know that I care about them and their future and more importantly that their teachers care about them. I want them to know that if they are dealt with a less-than-ideal life circumstance that they can get out and do big things, that there is hope, that they don't have to rely on the streets to get them through.

At the end of the day, it's about the kids. It's about keeping them inspired and motivated. I hope that I have a positive impact on them, because when it comes down to it, they absolutely have a positive impact on me.

On a typical inner-city school visit, Sherman asks the students how many want to play in the NFL. A fair number raise their hands. He asks them how many years does an average NFL career last. Students guess between five and ten years. Wrong, Sherman says, it is only three and a half years. For effect, he will pinch his forefinger and thumb together and then spread his 78-inch wingspan to illustrate how small an NFL career is compared to the rest of their lives. He urges students to get prepared and to avoid gang culture. He concludes, "It's tough out there. But once you make it out, nobody can stop you … If you can make it here, you can make it anywhere."

Coach Sherman

Without question, Sherman is a huge asset on game day, but he is also a huge asset behind the scenes. As a teammate, Sherman is determined to help everyone succeed. During practice, he assumes the role of an unofficial assistant coach and points out ways pass receivers and his fellow defensive backs can improve their play. Being so cerebral and maniacal about reviewing film, he is a natural at teaching the rest of the team about opponents and their game plans. He also gives extra attention to rookies and newcomers. His mentorship not only strengthens the Seahawks as a whole, but it also develops bonds between new players and veterans. True, it is not uncommon for veterans to mentor new players, but Sherman goes the extra mile. When someone needs more practice, Sherman comes in early and stays late. "He's selfless," says young receiver Tyler Lockett. "You don't really see that in a lot of people, especially who have had as much success as him. He's willing to stay after and help people, regardless if they're on the first team or on the practice squad … The things he does on a daily basis kind of shocks you. It is rare to see a player of his ability and his accomplishments being willing to sacrifice for the greater good, just to help somebody be better."

Blanket Coverage

Not being drafted until the fifth round was particularly painful to Sherman. However, the perceived insult did not prevent him from acknowledging his own worth and recognizing his intention to be a better person. From the start, Sherman knew he had something to share with students, especially student athletes, in Compton, Watts, and other neighborhoods where poverty and gang influences were prevalent.

On one of his visits to Dominguez High School, Sherman was in the gym and saw a student who played on the football team wearing cleats while lifting weights. Granted, the student had been able to come up with cleats to wear on the playing fields, but he could not afford an additional pair of shoes to wear indoors. "Seeing that, that's when you want to give back," Sherman has said. "You want to find a way to get shoes on his feet so he can separate himself from the weight room to the field. You can't be in there lifting with cleats on, it's just not safe."

Many students in the inner city, such as that young athlete, are trying to achieve despite their many obstacles. Sherman recognizes their determination and actively and personally supports them. He has said, "There are kids out there just trying to find a way. They don't have much and they're working with what they have. You've got to appreciate that. But also, in my heart of hearts, I want to make a better situation for them." Sherman decided to form a nonprofit foundation to mentor and support students.

It is not common for a player on a rookie's salary to establish such a program, but Sherman was raised to be generous and compassionate. Speaking of his parents, he said, "They've always emphasized treating people right, showing empathy regardless of what their circumstances are. If they're homeless, down on their luck, my parents would open their house to them, feed them, give them whatever they could to help them out, because they're good

Richard Sherman Scorecard

Amateur Achievements: Named *USA Today* All-American for winning California state track and field title in the triple jump (2005); receives Pac-10 All-Freshman Honors and Sporting News' Freshman All-American Honors (2007); accepts a football scholarship to play at Stanford University (2005).

Professional Achievements: Pro Football Writers All-Rookie First Team (2011); Associated Press NFL All-Pro, Pro Football Writers First Team, Pro Football Focus First Team (2012–16). named to the Pro Bowl (2013–2016); leads NFL in interceptions (2013); named NFC Defensive Player of the Year (2014); receives NFL 101 Award as one of four players recognized for outstanding achievement (2014); wins Super Bowl with Seattle (2014).

Honors: Named Dominguez High School Salutatorian, GPA 4.2. (2006); wins Best Breakthrough Athlete ESPY Award given to greatest breakthrough athlete in a major international individual sport or North American professional team sport (2014); selected as cover athlete for Madden 2015 video game; wins Steve Largent Award given to the Seahawks player who "best exemplifies the spirit, dedication, and integrity of the team; receives Pro Football Writers Good Guy Award given to the player who provides media with the most insightful interviews; in the 2016 top ten of *Sports' World's* "Most Charitable Athletes," *DoSomething.org's* "Athletes Gone Good" (annual list of the world's most charitable sports stars), and *Bleacher Report's* "Top Ten Most Awesomely Generous Sports Stars on the Planet."

people … You should always try to help people, and you should hope that if you're ever in that situation, people would try to help you."

The foundation that Sherman formed—Blanket Coverage, The Richard Sherman Family Foundation—has been active since 2013. Its mission is to provide students in low-income communities with school supplies, up-to-date textbooks and materials, adequate clothing, and sports equipment, such as cleats, helmets, or baseball gloves, giving them the basic necessities to achieve their goals. "I feel obligated to make the inner city a better place," he said. "We shouldn't ever leave a kid behind. But it's hard for them to take the SATs when the textbooks they're using were made in 2000. How can they compete?"

Each winter, during the holiday season, Sherman plays Santa. It began the winter after he was drafted, when he decided to adopt a family for Christmas. In the years following, he chose twenty-five families, twenty-five being his jersey number. In 2016, after reviewing recommendations from social agencies and elementary schools, Sherman found it too difficult to select only twenty-five families, and instead chose thirty-eight families in need. His fiancée, Ashley Moss, who grew up in the same neighborhood where some of the chosen families live, contacted the families and received both a wish list and a needs list. Then she went shopping, making several trips and filling up dozens of shopping carts with gifts and supplies. On the week before Christmas, the foundation hosted a party for the families at the Seahawks practice field, with many of his teammates attending. Sherman donned his Santa suit and passed out the presents. Said Moss, "It's amazing. Every year, it's just more and more of a blessing to be able to share our blessings and see this grow.

It doesn't get old to see the tears, to see the joy, to see the happiness, to see the kids running around and meeting guys they look up to. It can be life-changing."

Play Ball

Sherman is more than aware that professional athletes have a major impact on people, especially young people in the community. One of the most entertaining events that his foundation sponsors is a celebrity softball game, which has been held in July since 2013. Thousands of fans fill the bleachers at the Seattle Mariners' ballpark to donate to the foundation and watch some of their favorite celebrities clown around and play softball.

Sherman plays defense during a junior training camp for about 250 children that was put on by the Kennewick High School (WA) coaching staff.

Sherman playfully argues with All-Pro receiver and former teammate Golden Tate over a "bad call" by referee Lance Easley in Sherman's Blanket Coverage Foundation charity celebrity softball game.

Richard Sherman: Shutting Down and Speaking Up

The game is held in the offseason, so it is a testament to Sherman's popularity that these stars take time away from their personal lives to come and play. It is always an amusing contest, as most haven't played baseball since Little League. The exception is quarterback Russell Wilson, who played in college well enough to be drafted by the Texas Rangers. Besides teammates Michael Bennet, Doug Baldwin, Cliff Avril, Kam Chancellor, Thomas Rawls, Jermaine Kearse, and Earl Thomas, celebrities include former and current NFL pros such as Larry Fitzgerald, Terrell Owens, Lawyer Malloy, and Odell Beckham, Jr.; basketball players Nate Robinson, Jamal Crawford, Shawn Kemp, Kevin Durant, and Kobe Bryant; and musicians Macklemore and Snoop Dogg.

The money raised pays for school supplies and sports equipment for students in need. Said Seattle resident Jamal Crawford, "When we can all come together and do something positive, something lasting, I think it's pretty cool." Sherman is grateful for, and in his words humbled by, their support, explaining: "All our efforts are focused towards making sure the next generation has a better chance."

Pete Carroll calls Sherman "an extraordinary guy." Sherman is thankful to him and all the others who have believed in him along the way. "This game has given me the ability to live my dreams. We all know what we signed up for, and despite all the negatives, this game has allowed me to take care of my family in ways I never thought possible and to give more back to my community than I could have ever dreamed. I'm grateful for everything football has given to me."

Timeline

March 30, 1988 Born in Compton, California to Kevin and Beverly Sherman.

February 1, 2006 Accepts a football scholarship and admission to Stanford University, signing letter of intent.

June 2006 Graduates from Compton's Dominguez High School with a 4.2 GPA.

2006–2007 Leads Stanford's receivers in receptions.

September 2008 Knee injury forces Sherman to sit out for the rest of the season; he receives a medical redshirt so he can play two more seasons in college.

Spring 2009 Transitions from wide receiver to cornerback for Stanford.

June 14, 2010 Receives his Bachelor of Arts degree in communications with a 3.9 GPA.

April 30, 2011 Seattle selects Sherman in the fifth round of the NFL Draft, 154th overall.

October 30, 2011 Makes his first NFL start at cornerback against Cincinnati and makes his first interception.

October 14, 2012 Intercepts quarterback Tom Brady in an upset of the Patriots. Brady and Seahawks exchange taunts. Sherman posts photo, tweets "U mad, Bro?"

December 9, 2012 Scores his first NFL touchdown on a nineteen-yard interception return.

December 23, 2012 Returns a blocked punt ninety yards for a touchdown against the San Francisco 49ers.

September 29, 2013 Returns an interception fifty-eight yards for a touchdown late in the fourth quarter to tie the Houston Texans, despite losing one shoe.

2013 Founds Blanket Coverage, The Richard Sherman Family Foundation.

December 29, 2013 Finishes the regular season with an NFL-best eight interceptions.

January 19, 2014 Tips last-second pass thrown to 49ers receiver Michael Crabtree in the end zone. The ball is intercepted, sealing victory in the NFC Championship game and a trip to the Super Bowl. Delivers outspoken interview with sideline reporter Erin Andrews. Declares himself "best corner in the game," and defames Crabtree, setting off a national controversy.

February 2, 2014 Seahawks win their first Super Bowl by beating the Denver Broncos, 43–8.

May 7, 2014 Signs four-year contract extension for $57 million.

February 1, 2015 Seahawks lose Super Bowl XLIX to New England Patriots, 28–24. Sherman runs across the field to be the first to shake Tom Brady's hand.

December 20, 2016 Named to fourth consecutive Pro Bowl.

Glossary

All-Pro A football award given to players who are the best at their positions. The highest rated organizations that cast votes are the Associated Press, Pro Football Writers Association, and Pro Football Focus.

backpedal A technique especially important for cornerbacks, requiring running backward, keeping shoulders over the toes, and pumping arms. Allows for quick turning.

blitz A defensive play in which a linebacker or defensive back leaves his normal responsibilities in order to rush the quarterback to sack him or pressure him to throw too quickly.

bubble screen A pass play on which a receiver retreats into the backfield and runs wide behind a grouping of blocking receivers. A cornerback must abandon coverage on a receiver, burst through the bubble, and tackle the ball carrier.

conscientious objector A person who refuses to serve in the military based on moral or religious reasons.

cornerback A defensive back who covers pass zones on the outer edges of the field or who does one-on-one coverage of a wide receiver lined up at the outer edge of a formation.

defensive backs Players in the defensive backfield, including a free safety, a strong safety, left and right cornerbacks, and sometimes a dime back and nickel back. Dime backs and nickel backs are used when offenses use more than two wide receivers.

depth chart A weekly list drawn up by coaches that lists which players will start and which will be reserves who rotate in or replace a starter due to injury or poor performance.

4-3 alignment A defensive formation that sets up four linemen along the line of scrimmage, three linebackers behind and four defensive backs, usually two cornerbacks and two safeties.

home field advantage The advantage an NFL team earns by posting the best record in its conference. This means the team plays all its postseason games at home until the Super Bowl.

meme An idea, behavior, style, theme, or use of language that spreads from person to person. On the internet, it is used to mean an amusing or interesting picture or video that spreads widely.

NFL Combine A weeklong invitational event in Indianapolis during which the best college football players perform physical and mental tests for NFL coaches, general managers, and scouts.

Pac-10 The Pacific-10 Conference, in the western United States, made up of the University of Arizona, Arizona State University, University of California–Berkeley, University of Oregon, Oregon State University, Stanford University, University of California–Los Angeles, University of Southern California, University of Washington, and Washington State University. In 2011, the league added the University of Colorado–Boulder and the University of Utah, to make it the Pac-12.

picks Football slang for an interception. A pick-six is an interception returned for a touchdown, which is good for six points.

pocket In football, a cup-shaped or U-shaped area formed by offensive linemen and running backs to protect the quarterback as he looks for an open receiver.

press coverage A defensive tactic in which cornerbacks line up near the line of scrimmage and try to aggressively interrupt the receiver's route; it is legal only within 5 yards of the line of scrimmage.

Pro Bowl All-star game held between the two conferences. Players are voted in by coaches, players, and fans. The game is held the week before Super Bowl.

punt Play where the offensive team kicks the ball to their opponents, usually after failing to advance the ball 10 yards on the previous three plays.

red zone The area on the field between the defensive team's 20-yard line and its goal line.

sack When a defensive player tackles the quarterback behind the line of scrimmage before the ball is thrown.

safety A defensive back usually not assigned to cover a specific receiver. A free safety covers the deep part of the field, and assists a targeted cornerback in defending a pass. A strong safety lines up closer to the line of scrimmage, either to cover a tight end, who is a larger, stronger pass receiver, or to defend against the run.

secondary The group of defensive backs, usually safeties and cornerbacks. Also, the term is used to describe the medium-to-deep area where these players normally line up.

shutdown cornerback A defensive back who is able to severely restrict the effectiveness of star wide receivers.

slot The gap between the end of the offensive line and a wide receiver. A slot receiver lines up in this gap behind the line of scrimmage. The slot defensive formation puts a third cornerback across from that receiver in man-to-man coverage.

tight end An offensive player who usually lines up close to the end of the offensive line and can act as either a pass receiver or a blocker.

turnovers In football, any play in which the defense takes possession of the football away from the offense, either by fumble or interception.

wild card round Six teams in each conference qualify for the postseason. The two division winners in each conference with the best records sit out this round, which pits the other two division winners against the two wild card teams.

wingspan The distance between the tip of a player's middle finger, across the chest to the tip of the other middle finger when the player's arms are spread wide.

zone defense The responsibility of defending a specific area of the field. A cornerback in zone coverage must remain in his assigned zone and not follow receivers who pass through it.

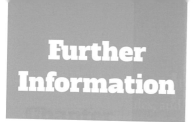

Further Information

Books

Carroll, Pete. *Win Forever: Live, Work, and Play like a Champion.* New York: Portfolio Penguin, 2011.

Frederick, Shane. *Side-by-Side Football Stars: Comparing Pro Football's Greatest Players.* North Mankato, MN: Capstone Press, 2014.

News Tribune. *Super Hawks: The Seattle Seahawks' 2013 Championship Season.* Chicago: Triumph Books, 2014.

Turner, Mark Tye. *Seattle Seahawks Super Season: Notes from the Best Season in Seahawks History.* Seattle: Sasquatch Books, 2014.

Websites

My Cause; My Cleats—Seattle Seahawks

www.seahawks.com/ms/mycleats

During week 13 of the 2016 season, Richard Sherman and some other Seahawks wore customized footwear to represent their charitable causes.

NFL Player Profile Page Richard Sherman

www.nfl.com/player/richardsherman/2495507/profile

The official NFL profile page gives stats, awards, and links to articles and videos.

Player's Tribune: "Tuesdays with Richard on Thursdays."

www.theplayerstribune.com/category/richard-sherman-tuesdays-on-thursdays

Richard Sherman's online column for the Player's Tribune, in which he writes on a variety of topics from charitable giving, education, NFL rules, racism in sports, and teamwork.

Richard Sherman #25

www.richardsherman25.com

"I'm just a guy trying to be the best, to help his team win, and who goes out there and puts his life and passion into his work," says Richard Sherman on his website's homepage. The website includes a bio, stats, blog, and information about his foundation.

Richard Sherman—Seattle Seahawks

www.seahawks.com/team/players/roster/richard-sherman

The official Seattle Seahawks team player profile. Includes stats, a bio, game day photos, and videos.

Video Links

Best of Richard Sherman

www.youtube.com/watch?v=8IXMKH13pt8

The NFL's "Best NFL Players Club" shows highlights of cornerback Richard Sherman's interceptions and entertaining interviews.

Get to Know Richard Sherman: The Trash-Talking Cornerback

www.youtube.com/watch?v=JjZzyhBYe-4
This eleven-minute production from NFL Films talks about how Richard Sherman's tough upbringing inspired him to be a great athlete and a great person.

Richard Sherman vs. Michael Crabtree: The Swat Heard Around the World

www.youtube.com/watch?v=OhtfaME_v0Y
This NFL official video covers Richard Sherman game-saving play against the San Francisco 49ers and his encounter with Michael Crabtree.

Who is Richard Sherman?

www.youtube.com/watch?v=pLDHy0HrzIs
Interview with Richard Sherman by sportswriter Kenny Mayne shows the sides of Richard Sherman many do not know—of a warm, generous, and thoughtful person.

Bibliography

Books

Turner, Mark Tye. *Seattle Seahawks Super Season: Notes from a 12 on the Best Season in Seahawks History*. Seattle: Sasquatch Books, 2014.

Online Articles

Asher, Matthew. "Richard Sherman Makes Things Go BOOM!" CBS. August 28, 2014. http://newyork.cbslocal.com/2014/08/28/richard-sherman-makes-things-go-boom.

Boyle, John. "Seahawks Cornerback Richard Sherman 'The Epitome Of A Team Guy.'" Seattle Seahawks. October 7, 2016. http://www.seahawks.com/news/2016/10/07/seahawks-cornerback-richard-sherman-%E2%80%9C-epitome-team-guy%E2%80%9D.

Brewer, Jerry. "Can You Hear Richard Sherman Now?" *Seattle Times*. January 12, 2013. http://www.seattletimes.com/sports/can-you-hear-richard-sherman-now.

Coates, Ta-Nehisi. "Richard Sherman's Best Behavior." *Atlantic*. January 20, 2014. https://www.theatlantic.com/entertainment/archive/2014/01/richard-shermans-best-behavior/283198.

Drovetto, Tony. "Reliving Richard Sherman's 28 Career Picks on His 28th Birthday." March 30, 2016. http://www.seahawks.com/news/2016/03/30/reliving-richard-shermans-28-career-picks-his-28th-birthday.

Dyce, Mike. "Richard Sherman's HS Coach Says He Was like Terrell Owens." FanSided. January 22, 2014.

http://fansided.com/2014/01/22/richard-shermans-hs-coach-says-like-terrell-owens.

Farmer, Sam. "Seattle Seahawks' Richard Sherman Is a Hit at Compton Alma Mater." *Los Angeles Times.* April 1, 2015. http://www.latimes.com/sports/nfl/la-sp-richard-sherman-compton-dominguez-20150402-story.html.

Jenkins, Lee. "Smacktalk Poet Richard Sherman Delights in Getting on Others' Nerves." *Sports Illustrated.* January 20, 2014. http://www.si.com/nfl/2014/01/20/richard-sherman-seattle-seahawks.

Kiebus, Matt. "23 Reasons Richard Sherman Is Actually One of the Most Likable Players in The NFL." *BuzzFeed.* January 24, 2014. https://www.buzzfeed.com/mjkiebus/23-reasons-richard-sherman-is-quietly-one-of-the-most-likabl?bftw&utm_term=.vnQp6lOy7#.do6vyV3ex.

Klemko, Robert. "Richard Sherman Is Showing He's Straight Outta Compton … and Stanford." FOX Sports. January 5, 2017. http://www.foxsports.com/nfl/story/nfl-playoffs-richard-sherman-seattle-seahawks-010517.

Manfred, Tony. "Richard Sherman's Brilliant Advice for High School Football Players." *Business Insider.* January 21, 2014. http://www.businessinsider.com/richard-sherman-high-school-football-advice-2014-1.

Merrill, Elizabeth. "In Seattle, the Secondary Comes First." ESPN. January 10, 2014. http://www.espn.com/nfl/playoffs/2013/story/_/id/10259323/nfl-playoffs-seattle-secondary-comes-first.

"Richard Sherman Career." National Football League. January 2017. http://www.nfl.com/player/richardsherman/2495507/careerstats.

"Richard Sherman Stats." Pro-Football-Reference. January 2017. http://www.pro-football-reference.com/players/S/SherRi00. htm.

Sherman, Richard. "How We Play Football in Seattle." *Players Tribune*. September 8, 2016. http://www.theplayerstribune.com/ richard-sherman-seahawks-how-we-play-football-in-seattle.

———. "Richard Sherman's Blog." https://www.richardsherman25. com/blogs/blog

Shpigel, Ben. "Seahawks' Richard Sherman Is Much More Than Just Talk." *New York Times*. January 25, 2014. https://www.nytimes. com/2014/01/26/sports/football/seahawks-richard-sherman-is-much-more-than-just-talk.html?_r=1.

Strauss, Valerie. "Justifying Richard Sherman by His GPA at Stanford." *Washington Post*. February 1, 2014. https://www. washingtonpost.com/news/answer-sheet/wp/2014/02/01/ justifying-richard-sherman-by-his-gpa-at-stanford/?utm_ term=.99d0af10352b.

Wilner, Jon. "Richard Sherman: What Makes Him Tick?" San Jose *Mercury News*. August 12, 2016. http://www.mercurynews. com/2014/01/19/richard-sherman-what-makes-him-tick.

Zirin, Dave. "Richard Sherman, Racial Coding and Bombastic Brainiacs." *Nation*. January 20, 2014. https://www.thenation. com/article/richard-sherman-racial-coding-and-bombastic-brainiacs.

Index

Page numbers in **boldface** are illustrations. Entries in **boldface** are glossary terms.

National Football League (NFL), 5, 9, 23, 36–37, 40, 42, 45, 51, 55, 57, 59, 62, 66, 71, 89, 91

NFC West, 52, 62

NFL Combine, 41, 42

Pac-10, 31, 40, 91

parents, 9–10, 13, **15**, 16–18, 21, 32, 35, 88, 92

picks, 20, 72

pocket, 55

press coverage, 43, 48, 66, 68

Pro Bowl, 54, 64, 68, 91

punt, 23, 25, 46

receiver, 20, 23–25, 30–36, 40, 42–43, 46, 50, 52, 55, 64–66, 68–69, 71, 73–74, 89–90

red zone, 66

sack, 25, 51, 72, 77

safety, 30, 44, 50, 55, 64, 68, 80

SATs, 17, 92

school performance, 6–7, 12, 17, 29, 73, 85

Seattle, 59, **63**, 71, 74, 77, **78**, 80, 85, 87

Seattle Seahawks, 5, 7, 9, 24, 40, 44–45, 48, 50–52, 54–55, 57–59, 62–66, 68–69, 71, 74, 77, 80–81, 90, 93

secondary, 7, 34, 55, 64–65, 69, 71

Shaw, David, 34, 87

Sherman Island, 64, 69

Sherman, Beverly, 9, 11–14, **15**, 16, 32, 44

Sherman, Branton, 9, 12–16, 18, 20, 30, 85

Sherman, Kevin, 9, 11–12, 14, **15**, 16, 18–19, 32, 44

shutdown cornerback, 58

slot, 48, 52, 69

Sports Illustrated, 63, 80

Stanford University, **22**, 29–32, **33**, 34–36, 40, 52, 56–57, 78, 85, 87, 91

Super Bowl, 14, 62, 65, 68, 71–74, 77, 80–81, 84, 91

Thomas, Earl, 50, 55, 64, 68–69, 85, 96

tight end, 23–24

track and field, 6, 20, 23–25, 30, 91

trash-talk, 7, 59, 64

turnovers, 51, 71

Ruth Bjorklund has a master's degree in library and information science. She has written numerous books for young people on a variety of subjects—science, wildlife, geography, history, and contemporary issues. She lives on Bainbridge Island, a ferry ride away from Seattle, Washington. The Seattle Seahawks are her team, and after a win, when the fireworks are set off in the stadium, she and her friends can see the display from the ferry dock.